D1712931

Feel Rooted

Being Connected

Reach Out!

Learning to overcome negative thoughts and stay mindful is not the same as fighting depression. Do you feel overwhelmed by sadness? Remember, you matter. You are not alone. If you need help, reach out. Talk to an adult you love and trust. This could be a teacher, school counselor, or family member. Make an appointment with your doctor. Seek professional help. Or call the National Suicide Prevention Lifeline at 1-800-273-8255. Someone is available to talk with you 24 hours a day, every day.

45TH PARALLEL PRESS

Published in the United States of America by Cherry Lake Publishing
Ann Arbor, Michigan
www.cherrylakepublishing.com

Reading Adviser: Marla Conn, MS, Ed., Literacy specialist, Read-Ability, Inc.
Book Designer: Melinda Millward

Photo Credits: © Hugo Felix/Shutterstock.com, back cover, 20; © George Rudy/Shutterstock.com, cover, 5;
© kuroksta/Shutterstock.com, 6, 14, 18; © FatCamera/istockphoto.com, 7; © calvindexter/Shutterstock.com,
8; © Momento Design/Shutterstock.com, 10; © Wachiwi/Shutterstock.com, 11; © Mehmet Hilmi Barcin/istock-
photo.com, 12; © Jacob Lund/Shutterstock.com, 13; © monkeybusinessimages/istockphoto.com, 15; © Svetog-
raphy/Shutterstock.com, 16; © Casper1774 Studio/Shutterstock.com, 19; © davooda/Shutterstock.com, 22;
© WAYHOME studio/Shutterstock.com, 23; © monkeybusinessimages/istockphoto.com, 24, 27; © Songquan
Deng/Shutterstock.com, 25; © Jacky Co/Shutterstock.com, 26; © Kwaczek/Shutterstock.com, 28;
© chaythawin/Shutterstock.com, 30

Graphic Element Credits: © kkoman/Shutterstock.com, back cover, front cover, multiple interior pages; © str33t
cat/Shutterstock.com, front cover, multiple interior pages; © NotionPic/Shutterstock.com, multiple interior pages;
© CARACOLLA/Shutterstock.com, multiple interior pages; © VikiVector/Shutterstock.com, multiple interior pages

45th Parallel Press is an imprint of Cherry Lake Publishing.

Library of Congress Cataloging-in-Publication Data has been filed and is available at catalog.loc.gov

Printed in the United States of America
Corporate Graphics

Table of Contents

INTRODUCTION

Have you ever felt a little off, like you're not yourself? It's important to feel **rooted**. Rooted means to feel like you belong. Connecting with others is a human need. We connect with family. We connect with friends. We connect with pets.

There are many ways to connect with others. We can connect in person. We can connect online. The key is to be open-minded. People need **communities**. A community is a group that shares something in common.

This book gives you tips on how to be **mindful**. Mindful means being aware. It means taking care of your body and mind. Take a moment. Practice being connected. Just breathe …

Tip: Choose to be connected.

CHAPTER ONE
Meditate to Relate

Meditation is deep thinking. It focuses the mind for a period of time. It's a way for your brain to relax. Sometimes this leads to your body relaxing as well. Meditation allows us to think more clearly. It helps us connect better.

Meditate every day. Do this for a few minutes. The best time to meditate is in the morning. Let yourself calm down. Recharge your body and mind. You'll be more creative. You'll be able to work more. It's good to meditate before bed too. You'll sleep better. You'll wake up refreshed.

Be mindful about your meditation. Focus on developing a deep sense of connection. Focus on the present moment.

Tip: Find a way to be silent. Be still for a little bit. Take a few minutes to collect yourself.

Find a quiet place. Be comfortable. You can do this exercise lying or sitting down. It helps to have someone slowly read this to you. Or you can record yourself reading this. Just play the recording when you want to meditate.

- Take deep breaths. Feel your body move with each breath.
- Think about where you're at. Connect with your bed or chair. Pay attention to the heaviness of sitting or lying down.
- Imagine yourself sinking further into the bed or chair. Remind yourself you're in a safe space.
- Imagine the earth rising up to hold you. Feel it giving you a big hug. Think about how the earth holds all living things in this way.
- Think of someone you'd like to hug in this way. Feel a sense of belonging and connection.
- Focus on your breathing again.

Tip: Think about how the earth is held in space. Think about connections to stars and planets.

Real-Life Scenarios

Life is full of adventures. There will be challenges. Things happen. Make good choices. These are some events you could face:

- You have been studying for days. You haven't talked to any of your friends in a while. How do you reconnect with your friends? What actions can you take?

- Your older sister has moved to college. You miss her. You've been texting. But you want to hear her voice. You have tried calling her. But you keep missing her phone calls. What can you do? How can you connect with her?

- You are on a family trip. You forgot your phone. How do you feel? What will you do? How can you make do without it?

CHAPTER TWO
Disconnect to Connect

Technology is all around us. We are connected to our **devices**. Devices include phones, tablets, and TV. Don't replace human contact with devices.

Take a tech break. Too much screen time is not good. It can cause a lot of health problems. It can also make you feel detached from reality.

Challenge yourself to **disconnect**. Disconnect means to turn off devices. It means logging off social media.

- Take a trip somewhere. Don't take your devices.
- Try "**Mellow** Mondays." Mellow means to be relaxed. On Mondays, try living without one form of technology.

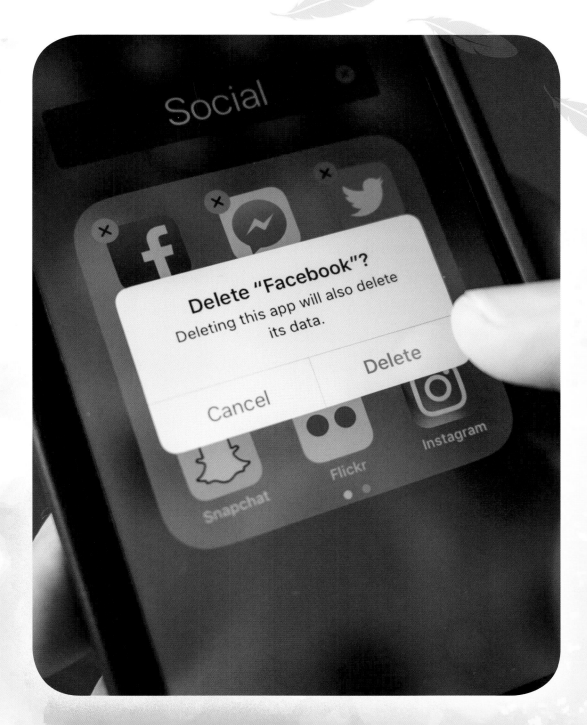

Tip: Clean out your technology every few months. Delete apps. Delete pictures from your phone. Get rid of the clutter.

There are many things you can do while disconnected.

- Instead of texting, invite a friend out. Go for a walk. Meet for a bite to eat. Chat in real life.
- Instead of commenting on posts, call a friend. Talk to people in person.
- Instead of posting pictures, take silly pictures with your friends. Print the pictures, and host a **scrapbooking** party. A scrapbook is a blank book that is filled with clippings or pictures.
- Instead of video chatting, play! Go outside. Play tag. Play sports. Dance.
- Instead of playing video games, play board games. Take a break from the television or computer screen.
- Instead of watching videos or movies, do something. Read a book. Write a play and act it out. Make art.

Tip: Put your charger in a different room. Don't have it by your bed. Start your morning without a tech check.

CHAPTER THREE
Be Present During Conversations

To **converse** means to talk with other people. Conversations are the best way to connect. People talk about interesting things. They share ideas. They share feelings. They share thoughts. This sharing makes us feel connected.

Mindful conversing means being present during conversations. Give the speaker all of your attention. Be a good listener. Be a good friend.

Put away your devices. Don't text while someone is talking. This is rude. It means you're not in the present moment. You're somewhere else. Give your attention to the speaker.

Tip: Avoid distractions. Pick a space that allows for good conversation.

Be aware of how you are listening. There are many ways to let the speaker know you are engaged.

- Make eye contact.
- Ask questions.
- Say the speaker's name. Do this several times in the conversation. This will help you remember names. This will also help the speaker feel welcomed.
- Remember key points.
- Make sure you understand what the speaker said.
- Thank the person for conversing. Thank them for sharing.
- Make future plans. Ask for updates about the things you've talked about.

Tip: Sometimes, you might feel like you don't have anything to talk about. Ask questions. People like talking about themselves and sharing stories. This can be a good way to break the ice.

Science Connection

Mammals are warm-blooded animals. They have hair or fur. They feed milk to their young. Humans are mammals. Dr. Harry Harlow lived from 1905 to 1981. He was an American psychologist. His most famous study was about monkeys and their mothers. He worked with rhesus monkeys. These monkeys are like humans. Harlow took the babies away from their mothers. He did tests. He found that touch is very important for making connections. The baby monkeys who didn't leave their mothers were healthier. Michael Kraus studied basketball players. He found players who touched each other more on the court won more games. Touch is the main way we communicate. It's how we feel safe. It's how we calm down. It's related to trust and love. Scientists have found that hugs have many positive benefits. Hugs make animals and people healthier and happier. Hugs help others connect.

CHAPTER FOUR
Be Mindful of Your Reputation

Your **reputation** is all that you truly own in this world. Reputation is what people think of you. It's what you're known for. People count on you. Your word is your honor. Your honor is in your control. You can make or break your reputation.

Be mindful of your reputation. Ask yourself:
- What do I want people to think of me?
- What are my strengths and weaknesses? How can I improve?

Do what you say you'll do.
- Meet your **deadlines**. Deadlines are when things need to be done.
- Do your best work. Take pride in your work. Don't turn in sloppy work.

7

8

14

15

Deadline.

21

22

28

29

Tip: Has someone asked you for help? It's okay to say no.

Be where you say you'll be. Nothing breaks a connection like not showing up.

- Be on time. Being late means you don't care.
- Show up for any plans you make.

There are times when you're too tired to go out. You may feel like skipping out on events. That's okay. Sometimes you need to recharge. Sometimes you need to take care of yourself first. Think about the following questions:

- Did I say I would go?
- Is my friend counting on me?
- Is my friend excited about the event?
- Did my friend put in time and effort to plan the event?

If you answered yes to any of these, then you should go. Put yourself in your friend's shoes. But don't go if you think you'll be in a bad mood. Don't go if you think you can't be present and engaged with your friend.

Tip: If something unexpected comes up, let your friend know right away that you will be late.

Spotlight Biography

Eleanor Roosevelt lived from 1884 to 1962. She was the wife of President Franklin D. Roosevelt. She was a strong leader. She did many things for human rights. She came from an important family. Her uncle was President Theodore Roosevelt. Roosevelt knew a lot of people. She supported many people. For example, she promoted Amelia Earhart, Marian Anderson, and others. Her influence paved the way for social justice. She was very active in the community. She has worked for the Red Cross. She joined the Women's Trade Union League. She joined the League of Women Voters. She was an active member of the Democratic Party. She founded and taught at a girls' school in New York. She was a delegate in the United Nations. She hired many women workers in the White House. She wrote a newspaper column. She spoke at many events. She also traveled the world. She met with many world leaders. She was well-connected.

CHAPTER FIVE
Get People Together

Create chances for people to connect. Be mindful as you make plans.

- Think about who you'd like to invite. Include as many people as you can. Don't leave people out. Try not to hurt people's feelings.
- Pick a place. Make sure the space is safe. Make sure the place is big enough. Create a **vibe**. Vibes are moods. Decorate to create this vibe.
- Think about the goal. Why do you want to host this? Why is building this connection important to you? What will you get out of it? What will others get out of it?

·········➤ **Tip**: Be careful of taking group selfies. Don't choose to include some people and not others.

There are many ways to get people to meet up.

- Host a book club. Have everyone read the same book.
- Host a movie club. Have everyone watch the same movie.
- Host a dance party. Put on some music. Dance your heart away! Do dance contests.
- Host a games night. Play different games.
- Host a camping trip. Go out in nature. Sleep in tents. Make a campfire. Tell scary stories.
- Host a **slumber** party. Slumber means to sleep. People can come over. They can spend the night.

Tip: Prepare discussion questions before your events. Be ready!

CHAPTER SIX
Say "Thank You"

Showing **gratitude** is the key to successful friendships. Gratitude means being thankful. Practice being thankful. Be mindful about it.

- Notice how many times you say "Thank you" in a day. Do you say it too much? Do you say it too little?
- Notice how you feel when you say "Thank you." Do you really mean it? Is it easy for you to say? Is it hard for you to say?
- Challenge yourself to say one real "Thank you" each day. Stop a moment before you say it. Think about why you are grateful. Then say, "I'd like to thank you for …"

Tip: Practice saying "I'm sorry." Be mindful about what that phrase means.

Thanking people shows that you value them. It makes people feel good. It builds connections. Handwriting thank-you notes can be a mindful activity. Writing these notes will make you think about gratitude. You have to focus on this task. That means you can't check your devices. Here are some tips for writing thank-you notes:

- Write the note as soon as possible.
- Include specific details. Share how you benefited.
- Make it personal.
- Send it through the mail. This shows you took time and effort.

Tip: Send a thank-you video.

Fun Fact

Chris Dancy is known as the "most connected man in the world." He uses a lot of technology. Some of it he wears! He has 300 to 700 tech systems running all the time. These systems capture data about his life. He even sleeps on a special bed. The bed is a computer system. It tracks his sleep. Even his dogs are tracked! Numbers rule his life. He's always checking in. He got connected because he wanted to keep better health records. He was also afraid of the internet shutting down. He didn't want to lose any of his work. He said, "I've lost 100 pounds (45 kilograms) and learned to meditate. I'm much more aware of how I respond to life and take steps to adjust to my environment. I've also formed better habits thanks to the feedback I'm getting."

HOST YOUR OWN MINDFULNESS EVENT!

Feeling out of the loop? Missing your friends? Needing to connect with others? This might be the best time to host your own mindfulness event! Help get people talking. Host a "Be Connected" Party!

STEP ONE: Figure out where you can host your party.

STEP TWO: Make invitations—and get creative! Ask a friend to help you. Send out the invitations.

STEP THREE: Plan your activities and get supplies.

Human Knot!

- Have no more than 10 people in a group.

- Tell everyone to stand shoulder to shoulder. Tell them to stand in a circle.

- Tell everyone to reach across the circle. Have them hold hands with two other people. They may not hold hands with people to their left or right. They're making a human knot.

- Have everyone untangle themselves without letting go of each other's hands. The goal is to stand next to the people whose hands they're holding.

- Encourage people to talk to each other. Encourage them to work as a team.

Crack a Smile!

- Have everyone stand in a circle.

- Choose someone to be in the middle. Tell this person their goal is to not smile or laugh.

- Tell everyone else their goal is to make the person in the middle laugh. Have everyone take turns. They can do anything except touch the person. They may make funny faces. They may tell jokes.

- Whoever makes the person in the middle smile or laugh switches places with that person.

Food Pairings!

- Give everyone a piece of paper.

- Tell everyone to write down their favorite food. It could be an appetizer. It could be a main dish. It could be a dessert.

- Have them draw a picture of the dish.

- Have everyone stand in a circle. Have everyone share their drawing.

- Tell everyone to choose a partner based on how well their food pairs together.

- Give each partner 3 to 5 minutes to talk about their food.

- Have everyone return to the circle. Have everyone share what they learned about their partner.

GLOSSARY

communities (kuh-MYOO-nih-teez) groups that share something in common

converse (kahn-VURS) to talk with other people in order to exchange ideas

deadlines (DED-linez) due dates

devices (dih-VISE-iz) tools that connect to technology like phones, tablets, and televisions

disconnect (dis-kuh-NEKT) to turn off from technology, devices, and social media

gratitude (GRAT-ih-tood) being thankful

meditation (med-ih-TAY-shuhn) deep thinking that involves focusing the mind for a period of time

mellow (MEL-oh) relaxed

mindful (MINDE-ful) focusing one's awareness on the present moment to center the mind, body, and soul

reputation (rep-yuh-TAY-shuhn) your worth or character as judged by other people

rooted (ROOT-id) feeling a sense of belonging

scrapbooking (SKRAP-buk-ing) filling a blank notebook with pictures and clippings

slumber (SLUHM-bur) sleep

vibe (VYBE) mood

INDEX

ABOUT THE AUTHOR

Dr. Virginia Loh-Hagan is an author, university professor, and former classroom teacher. She is a big advocate of writing thank-you notes. She lives in San Diego with her very tall husband and very naughty dogs. To learn more about her, visit www.virginialoh.com.